ALSO BY DAVE LORDAN

The Boy in the Ring (Salmon, 2007)
Invitation to a Sacrifice (Salmon, 2010)

salmonpoetry

DAVE LORDAN

Lost Tribe of the Wicklow Mountains

salmonpoetry

Published in 2014 by
Salmon Poetry
Cliffs of Moher, County Clare, Ireland
Website: www.salmonpoetry.com
Email: info@salmonpoetry.com

ISBN 978-1-908836-37-3

COVER IMAGE: Dave Lordan
COVER DESIGN & TYPESETTING: *Siobhán Hutson*
Printed in Ireland by Sprint Print

*Salmon Poetry gratefully acknowledges the support of
The Arts Council / An Chomhairle Ealaoín*

He would sometimes stop to gaze at a wall against which sick people had been for a long time discharging their spittle, and from this he would picture to himself battles of horsemen, and the most fantastic cities and widest landscapes that were ever seen; and he did the same with the clouds in the sky ... it may be said, in truth, that he changed his manner almost for every work that he executed.

VASARI ON DI COSIMO

Acknowledgments

Thanks as always to my family and friends, without whom nothing.

Thanks to Harry Clifton and the board of the Ireland Chair of Poetry for awarding me a bursary in 2011, providing a welcome morale boost and precious time in Annaghmakkerig to work on this book.

Thanks to Philip Coleman for continual and vital editorial support. Thanks to Sydney Weinberg for close reading and feedback. Thanks to Karl Parkinson, Peadar O'Grady, Stephen Murray, Rob Doyle, Ciarán Ó Ceallaigh and Bernard Clarke for their friendship, wisdom, and inspiration during the writing of this manuscript.

Thanks to the numerous event organizers who have invited me to present my work.

Thanks to the editors of the following magazines/websites/ programmes: *The Stinging Fly*, RTÉ Radio 1's *Arena*, Lyric FM's *Nova*, *Poetry International*, *Kluger Hans* (Belgium), *Poetry Bus Magazine*, *Irish Left Review* (print and online), *Southword*, *Burning Bush*, *Poethead*, *West Cork News*, *CrisisJam,* and *Minor Literatures.*

"I Dream of Crowds" appears in the anthology, *Shine On: Irish Writers For Shine*, published by Dedalus Press.

"When I was a Monk" was in *Berryman's Fate: A Centenary Celebration* published by Arlen House.

"Discover Ireland" was given away with sticks of rock by artist Augustine O Donoghue on the streets of Limerick in Autumn 2013, as part of the *Troubling Ireland* project.

Thanks to Jessie and Siobhán at Salmon Poetry.

In Memoriam Denis Boothman

Lost Tribe of the Wicklow Mountains

Contents

Lost Tribe of the Wicklow Mountains   13

Fertility Poem   15

Workmate   17

Hope   19

When I was a Monk   21

Lost Poem   23

Bees and The Authorities   25

Discover Ireland   27

Christine   29

Return of the Earl   31

Spin   33

I Dream of Crowds   35

Irish History   37

Notes for a Player   41

My Mother Speaks to Me of Suicide   61

Love Commands the Neighbourhood   64

Lost Tribe of the Wicklow Mountains

for Christy Moore

I believe in them, so they do exist.

In the Wicklow Mountains
It is easier to hide than you think.

Behind waterfalls.
In sunless crevices.
In densest rhododendroned foliage.

On slopes of fluttering shadow and scree.

Nothing I know of, apart from these lines,
Speaks of this tribe.

They might be waifs that escaped from
The lead-mines.

They might be vagrants who dropped
out of ballads and poems.

They might be rebels
Who outran the redcoats
Until the redcoats dissolved.

They might be ravers and Wiccans
who squat in high ruins
holding thousand day hooleys,
cavorting in roofless great halls.

They might change into foxes in moonlight
And paw through the motorway snow
To scavenge the exurban dustbins.

But, sincerely, this tribe has no patterns. It fits no descriptions.
Nothing about it – beyond its certain existence – translates:
No reason, no theses, no customs, no goal.

The tribe is my credo. That's all.

Strong is my faith.
Strong is my beat.
Strong is my magic.
Strong is my want

& wanting, I rise till
I'm vanishing with them,

Spinning in to a mist
Where I'll never be spotted
Above Mullaghcleevaun.

It's so righteous to stray.
It's so good to abandon.
It's so just to ascend
With the lost and forgotten

To summits the rooted
Cannot even imagine.

Fertility Poem

for Tina Pisco

Daa...aad, whaaaat... does... thaaaat... saaaaay, drawls Rosa,
trying out drawling today, after tweenie micro-stars
on Nickelodeon. She's pointing at graffiti

on the slats around the back of Superquinn.
It reads CUNT in dripping lipstick red.
I don't want to pronounce or define

CUNT for my six year old, so
COUNT's the proximate I play her with.
It says COUNT sweetie, COUNT.

She stares at CUNT, painstakingly mouthing
the letters so signs and sounds combine to sense
phonetically, as instructed to in Senior Infants.

Kuh-Uh-Enn-Tuh COUNT
Kuh-Uh-Enn-Tuh COUNT
Kuh-Uh-Enn-Tuh COUNT

Drawls. She's smart, well taught, doesn't
quite believe my lie that CUNT is COUNT.
Kuh-Uh-Enn-Tuh COUNT. Halts, alarmed, zipping

out of TV character: *Dad, that doesn't sound right.*
Around the alphabet we have shared an absolute trust;
I'm stumped – momentarily – then risk:

You know about silent letters, don't you, Rosa?
Letters that are there in the word when you spell it or write it
that you don't pronounce when speaking?

Uh-huh; she nods, gravely, eyes narrowing,
trying her damnedest to unravel
my unfamiliar spinning;

Well here is a case of an Invisible Letter,
a very unusual and almost magical thing,
which some call ghost, or even phantom letters.

What are you talking about, Dad?
A strange kind of letter you never see or say
in spelling out, but pronounce it anyhow, I tell her.

Like O in CUNT (which I pronounce Count).
Ok, Rosa says. This she can credit. It makes sense.
There are silent letters; why not invisibles?

Reconciled by such whitewash to our environment,
we dawdle on in thoughtful, mutual silences
past those cardboard jesters on horses on steroids

galloping out of the Bookmaker's looking glass.
Moments later, my daughter – innocent, spontaneous,
and targeted (living in our world, as Bataille

says of the animals, *like water in water*) – freezes
outside Pizza Hut, reeled in by the humungous
poster of a Wagon-Wheel Pepperoni: Extra Thick and Cheesy Crust;

Dad I'm hungry, really really hungry, Dad.
Really I am Dad. Can we get one of those?
Animal appetites inundate our wisdoms when they surge.

Though we may alter a course now and then in the flood
as now we have altered our language.
Only tinily and privately, I realise; and yet, from here on in,

round the back of Charlesland Superquinn,
CUNT is COUNT invisibly, for both of us.
Lies are the womb and the seed of us.

Their fertility is marvellous.

Workmate

She plays Farmville and pokes friends
on Facebook most of the day,

scans a few sites for celebrity gossip –
photos and headlines –

scrolling up and down independent.ie
every quarter of an hour or so.

At 15.10 she takes a break and lounges
for half an hour

with the other women on the scheme
eating brown soda with orange-and-duck-liver pate.

Then they sample black pudding
reheated from yesterday,

chomping fat and gut and gristle
over *CSI*, *Dragon's Den*, *American Idol*.

Each one has something well worked-out
to say about the royal wedding.

Later on, closing in on 5pm – the goal –
she rises and jacks up the Korean office stereo

for Shakira, almost dancing
the way back to her chair.

Leaves max vol on for the jingles
witching for Stout,

for *The Sound of Music*
in the Grand Canal Theatre,

for cut-price bananas,
for less-than-half-price toys,

two-for-one Rioja,
three mince-meats for a tenner,

for closing-down firesales
of repossessed furniture.

Some of these ads she has
auto-didactically

learned
the dubbing of,

the how-to-hum-along-to
and when the DJ's billion-kilometre tongue flicks

through the speaker
and into the room

to put a question to his nation:
whether it is right to cut the benefits

of those who refuse a reasonable
offer of employment?

she damn near leaps from her desk with her very soul giving answer,
damn near levitates in an ecstasy with her arms and legs spread out,

damn near crashes through the roof, ascending
to the satellites

and the space debris
screeching

Yes, Yes, of course it is Yes,
Yes, of course it is, Yes.

Hope

Hope, ya ould mutt, I hear yer in bits.
I heard somebody stomped on yer throat an' all ya can do now
    is grunt.
I heard six drunk jocks set ya on fire while ya wuz goofin'.
Ya ould trout! Ya look like ya wuz washed up in an oilspill.
There's only a seepin' raw hole in yer face
instead uv a nose since yer septum fell out. Yer still snortin' though.
Yuv more tracks than the DART. Yuv every disease known tuh rats.
Ya got herpes, shingles an' worms. Ya got flyswarms, maggots an' lice.
    Cockroaches
crawlin' all over ya groupthink *Tiocfaidh ár lá*.
St Vincin De Paul wud rejeck ya. Yud have Augustine out on
    the lock.
St Francis'd turn away yodellin'. This time it ain't jus' a scare ya
    might really be dyin'.
Even the French seem tuh have banned ya, blottin' yer puss
    with the law.
Yemen is bleedin' from multiple wounds tuh revive ya.
Mosly, here in zombied Ireland, I can't even see ya, yer such
    a famished fuckin' wraith.
Ya flicker in an' out uv the view, accept no particular shape,
    like steam from a pipe or a
backalley splodge that can't be washed off.
I know ya wanna give up. I know yer only hope may be tuh dissolve,
become a puddle or rock, sit it out for a new geological era.
I know yuv ten millin ex-loves tuh attend tuh in wrecks uv the deep,
coffin-ships an' u-boats an' steamships o' seaweed an' flutin' bones for ya.
I know yuv a hundurd millin virgin spouses pushin' up slums
an' high-tech factories from underneath the battlefields.
Tis tuh the dead we can never repay yud mos jusly return,
them that rose an' wuz crushed for yer dreamin', the manygod
that manytimes gave ya generation. But I ain't ready tuh let ya
go jus' yet. So get up. Get up. I said GET THE FUCK UP!
An' c'mere and give us a hug and give us a peck

on the cheek, and give us a drag on yer spliff.
I know how beat up an' used up an' ugly ya are
an' yer only visible when I ain't right-minded.
But tis senses that matter, tis vision an' touch.
I cudden do either if I cudden with you.
I cudden love nothin' if I cudden love you.

When I was a Monk

for Máighréad Medbh

When I was a monk or whatever it is that I was
for a breeze in the big wooded days out the west
there was only one book which I portioned aloud
to myself on a Sunday, cud-chewed the rest of the week.

For art and characters I lay on the moss-swaddled slab
of a thousand year Chief, watched shape-changing shapes
ceaselessly drift without plot, then dissolve in a sun
wheeling round to a moon that put me into a trance.

I saw thunderous battles in the Epicking stars.
There were no repeats. I was never bored. Weather
was my living music – unscorable, mercurial, diverse;
varying seasons of trees, birds, animals, grasses, insects, seas –

mutable wind's modulations of these; innumerable rains
on the tracks, on the lake, down on hives, down on huts,
down on limestone, on granite, on canopies, thatch…
Occasional monsoonish burstings that freshened the airs

and galvanised armies of ants. The river whose noises
were never the same. My own organic back catalogue.
Sometimes, passing by near a cliff or a bank, a man on
a skiff would be singing of his mother's death to his daughter.

Or she'd be laughingly singing of newborns to him.
That would do me for a year. I heard angels in Sessiles
and demons in Yew stands disputing my soul. What harm?
All who have souls are disputed and split. Soldierly

drumming from slopes near the fjord; from which
slope exactly, who knew? I couldn't care less.
No-one can rob from a man who has nothing to give
only brotherly silence in the fathomless silence of God.

Each Spring I would stroll a few days to the coast,
and heave out as deep and as cold as I could
– waking my bones and my joints for the Summer.
Among amiable porpoises I glid and I dove,

gargling along in their gargletalk, as if I were one
of their brood. Every August I stood in a meadow
of storms, my palms stretched up rod-height.
I was struck once or twice by magnificent lightning

from Gabriel's Horn. My brain bloomed like a desert
bush. I was nothing but fire in those instants.
One day I fished a blue baby girl from the lake.
I shrouded her in my own black rags. In guttering

shades of a grove on the bank, ululating wildly
to frighten off animals, I scooped out a grave
and I buried her, with all available ceremony.
For 25 years I did kneel there and weep there

whenever I happened to pass. Daily, I noticed
new curls to a bird cry, new insects I refused
pinning through with a name. Names are a hex
on God's bounty. Extinction begins with a name.

Above all I saw – but it was more than a seeing –
how the world stays unowned and unmarked
in its infinite business like an infinite song
only sung by itself inside its own hearing.

No matter who for five minutes yaks
in a vanishing tongue
of squaring a rood
in the flow of this world,

driving stakes through fire and flood.

Lost Poem

So, you're lost?
Me too.

But don't get downhearted.
Even nature is lost.

Not the Moon nor Omega
can tell where it is.

Sit down in my shade, draw
a breath and relax

but keep watch. Before long,
we'll be surrounded by Wolves.

Or maybe this time, for a change,
Alsatians will come. Or the three-jawed hell-dog.

Who knows – we may end up
devouring each other.

It happens. However,
I don't advise it.

My flesh has more maggots and ticks
than my stink would suggest.

You'd be certain to chuck.
Better empty than sick, right?

Endings are terrible, beginnings painted
in blood. In between it's all losing.

That's why angels have wings
and live in cornices

sculpting clouds from our dreams
and the smoke of ambitions.

Meanwhile, humans have whiskey and forceps
to tug them along and keep them from choking.

I'm hungry. Are those Wolves or Alsatians?
My counsel to you is to run for your life

and later, when you have time
during a pause in a clearing,

torch all your maps and your guides,
blank your address book

and smash your connections.
Your guides are all predators' menus.

and they will use your connections
to track you.

Who am I to instruct
a modern professional like you?

I'm poetry. I'm the thick
and endless forest of the lost.

The Moon and Omega and
all the prime numbers

weep as they wander around me
encountering suicide's ghosts.

I dwell in your hope and your failure
like angels,

though I'm lighter than they are
and care even less.

Bees and The Authorities

Solinus, on the authority of Camden,
incontrovertibly declares that there are no bees in Ireland.
Keating impugns both Camden and Solinus
stating *Such is the quantity of bees,*
that they are found not only in hives,
but even in the trunks of trees, and in holes in the ground.

Modomnoc the beekeeper, who was with St David in Wales,
was followed to Ireland by an adoring swarm of bees.

Writing in the 8th century, Bede, the so-called Venerable
opines *Hibernia ... et salubritate ac serenitate aerum*
... Diues lactis ac mellis insula ... Or, so Google tells us,
Ireland has a fine climate, and is a land rich in milk and honey.

In 1920 Benedictine Brother Adam hybridized the Buckfast Bee.
According to The Economist in 1996 Brother Adam was
unsurpassed as a breeder of bees. He talked to them,
he stroked them. He brought to the hives a calmness that,
according to who saw him work, the sensitive bees responded to.

The Buckfast Bee – Brother Adam's supreme though far
from only achievement as a breeder – is super-productive,
extremely fecund, resistant to disease and disinclined to swarm.
However, it cannot perform miracles.

Good St Bega could. She fled Ireland for Northumbria,
away from an enforced marriage to a Norwegian Prince.
There she founded the still-extant Cumbrian coastal village
of St Bees, pop 1,717, enrolled in the census of 2001.

Sometime after, although not too long after, 850AD, St Bega,
to gain the land on which to build her priory
from goading Lord Egremont, made it snow

three inches deep on Midsummer's Day. Yes, she made it snow three inches deep on Midsummer's Day, dispossessing Lord Egremont, as well as, presumably, seriously upsetting the bees as a consequence.

Discover Ireland

for Philip Coleman

And sometimes the line is moving so fast
the head-of-line guy with the electric stunner
doesn't have time
to stun the cow properly.

The cow shunts on down the line
dazed but alive
to the second man,
an Estonian, aged 54,
(sending money home
to see after the grandchild).
His task — to slit the cow's throat
as soon as the cow's been stunned unconscious
by the first man (from just outside Tirana) —
but an unstunned cow will throw a bovine tantrum
for its life against the second man,
kicking and bucking and butting
against the eighteen-inch blade,
even as the blood is being drawn.

Sometimes the struggle is so rough and prolonged
that the middle-aged man from Estonia
is forced to withdraw the blade
in order to steady or defend himself
and once or twice the bloody blade
falls and slops into the blood-and-offal river
on the factory floor,
where the man,
like all the men,
must seep the leather of his boots all day.

Despite the beast strength
and mindless courage of the cow

the second man, this precarious man
with precarious offspring,
always manages, eventually,
and even without halting the line
– which would lead to penalties
for everyone –
to open the throat from ear to ear.

Out floods the thick red life of a cow.

Always, the new dead cow is advanced
to the third man, 21, from northern Brazil.

At the end of each weekday the second man
is covered, head to toe, in hoof-shaped bruises.
Black-and-blue patches,
reminiscent of cowhide.

Christine

You come and go in a cloud and I know you
As well as your mother knows you. Better than any fiction.
With all my degrees I can conjure you up anytime
and in 98% of places, though not during hurricanes or solar flashes.
Crews must sometimes work all night
To maintain or repair our connection.
You have three lovers: Santa Claus, Nostradamus, Merlin.
A savage gang they are, and in great form.
High fives and winks and in-talk and much laughter.
Full of strange power, ominous wisdom.
Like belief or truth are no precondition for anything.
Manage the fantasy. Club together up on top. Split them.
Demonstrably, Christine, you enjoy and satisfy
All three of your heros. They find you adequate, for now.
Understanding you part of a practically infinite queue.
There is no need for any kind of courtship.
Everyone says more or less what a higher animal would.
The whole thing reminds me of Pompeii.
A future abstract may speak of unspoken
Agreements to mutually fossilise.
We fix and restrict each other in this posture,
In this attic. Meanwhile, a volcano squats outside
In old reality, the Cambrian. From what alone
Goes on between us here can be told a whole lot more.
Excavate the webcam and you might find yourself
A ragged child in a chromite mine. For when will
Books be responsible for the machines that produce them?
We are all but examples, I know.
Tending towards the one inexpressible consequence.
We don't need names to be going on with and this one isn't yours.
Mine is Rocky. Rocky Byrne, how are ya?
Christine, you keep on breaking into my poems
With an emergency broadcast addressed to my
~~cock and balls~~; excuse me – core organs.

We need all history's madmen to encounter
One another in the here and now. You are done
No obvious physical harm in this scenario. You perform
All the requisite roles with the required contractual smile.
Then they – by which I mean we – let go.
All this may contain some meaning for the rest of us.
The smile – it might as well be genuine. Isn't it?
I'm well and I'm sick and I want to believe in it.
A sincere grin on you would be a real guiltwasher.
You can in no sense be described as an agent.
Something passing through us all which simply
Must pass through, move on. That is everyone's excuse/
Occasion. I received an intimation that you are an orphan
Of some previous disaster, Chernobyl maybe,
Which means that I, the many, must be your father.

Return of the Earl

for Denyse Woods

I saw it happening in Bantry. Sometime during the July night
An atmospheric trigger went and Earth and everything caught

Out on it instantaneously froze to an immeasurable cold.
All pipes congealed. All signals died. All instruments ceased.

All ways became immediately impassable. No missile could launch,
No drone take off. All orders were suddenly meaningless.

All networks of power dissolved. Caoinkeen, Knockboy
And all the Shehy range were gleaming crystal peaks

Again, kaleidoscopes of splintered moon, candle-luminous
In misty drifts beneath the planet light – planets which like

Everything had lost their name, their post, their role in the plot,
Yet continued namelessly and plotlessly to revolve.

Bantry Bay was Bantry Berg with frozen waves and foam.
Frozen melancholic swans of glass – Oh Tchaikovskian apocalypse!

The swimming pool was an eerie opaque cube, a chlorinated rink;
St Fin Barres' fractured spike an icy dagger in the gale;

The bins in rows in the square a fleeing tribe that turned to salt.
The only colour to look back upon was white. White on

White on snowblind white. The market house of white. The whitened
Millwheel at the library of white. Four Star Hotel White.
    The white lounge,

The playground white, the trawlers white, the Big White House.
Then it blizzarded a glacier down, it snowed a flood of snow.

Inch by inch, then foot by foot, the figures of St Brendan,
    Wolfe Tone and
The Spirit of Love were buried by the fall and disappeared.

It hailed – stones the size of satellites, stones the size of Neptune's
Little moons, for days, for weeks, for months, although there were

No clocks, there were no days, there were no months.
Bantry preserved – until the next epochal gyre – Hyberborean
    Pompeii.

But Humankind is hard as guilt or history to kill. One man overcame;
A diving instructor with an oxygen store and a butane supply,

Donning wool and furs over deep-sea diving gear, he cooked his nearest
Deep-freeze neighbours first, then his cats, and then his wife;

Used a gas-torch of his own design to tunnel a well-in-reverse,
Climbing and hacking and hauling and puffing until finally he burst

The seal, sucked the flowing tap of air and, propelled by a perpetual
    desire,
Struck out across the permafrost to uncover who still moves and talks

And hunts in County Cork, who's in charge now, what instructions are.

Spin

for Helen Lindstrom

Shhsssh! Silence is talking. Silence is driving the car.
She is neutral and she disapproves of all the gloom.
What have you got to be so angry about?
Would you just shut-up about the budget?
Nice things, why can't we just talk about nice things?
The lovely hedgerows and lawns hereabouts. Butterflies.
Our far flung children, high achievers all.
Old country recipes. Recent sporting victories.
Weddings we have been to. Other public ceremonies.
Our childhood in terms of its thoroughbred horses. The weather.
The good local weather. Which is not strange.
Stunned and fuming in the backseat, you and I
Being placed and viewed and spoken through like archaeology.
We are fragments in a carton. Ashes in an urn.
I wish that my container keeps a coiled snake
And a curse-bearing hieroglyph in it, that yours is an aboriginal wand.
Shhssh! Silence is priming her lashes, flinting her smile,
Cocking her teeth in the rear-view mirror.
They ricochet and crack us both mid-forehead,
Fester in our brainwaves like eyes, like thrones and sceptres,
like all the stations of the radio. We are monsters now.
But this is not what silence calls a crisis.
She would like to know exactly what our real problem is?
Are you workshy? Or perhaps it's S.A.D.
Deal with it. Get a goddamn job like the rest of us.
Go and sit under a stone-apple tree or swallow
A Halogen lamp for yourself. Go get electrocuted.
Go piss on electric wire. Didn't you hear about Berlin?
Don't you know how much worse it gets
A thousand years ago? Silence takes her holidays
In surgical resorts and has also the world's most
Incredible dentist, a true dambuilder. Shhssh!
Silence is only just paring the obvious:
Detrital, byproducted hope is foam and it is cornerless.

It boils away with heat and age like alcohol, like milk.
Get doom, solidify, welcome to the real world, get a fucking grip.
Shhssh! Silence floats about the sixties seeing it all before
And whatever you think is going on back then it doesn't happen.
It never ever. Silence do solemnly declare:
I am the national peaceful unity co-operation thingy.
I am fog on the lough, erasing shapes, maps, directions, memory.
I am *the calm that has settled after all hope has died*. *
I am the broken promises factory skirting every Irish town.
I am the Hotel Empty. My rating is five black-holes.
I host the most magnificent cobwebs, prestigious cracks,
glittering slug-trails, drafts of international importance.
You are very welcome to attend my International Emptiness
        Conference.
I am a warehouse of the unrequired. Defective mannequins.
I am the vastest hangar in all of limbo, that one for the
        unexamined.
I am the cage that traps the song, unbeknownst to the singer.
I am the code and the guard and the museum of the future.
Shhssh! Silence is driving us down to the pier.
Shhssh! Silence is dragging us onto the yacht.
Shhssh! Silence is taking us out on the lake.
Shhssh! Silence is packing us up in a jar,
Diving us down to her black, uninhabited realm,
Roots that throttle us in wrecks, grey silt-weeds
And the drifting, boneless dead, their softening shells.

* Hannah Arendt

I Dream of Crowds

I dream of crowds, in different guises.
I dream of drunken orgiastic crowds on sandy cliffs and beaches.
The aboriginal sun never falling. Everyone wearing the sun as a crown.

I dream a crowded DART, a mile-long DART
snaking through a bombed-out Cork,
past blazing stacks on Wexford hills,
through cratered Dublin exurbs,

and the passengers all dressed in sackcloth rags,
a sorry exodus with overspilling suitcases
in glazed-eye shock that seems enchantment,
squat on seatless carriages

all hypnotic concentration on
one missing infant's undulating wail
that never stops.

I dream a carnival crowd from my primary years.
Feral chaws in stripes and masks
picting through my childhood town,

provoking for sport
the well-primed hate
of other, crushed inhabitants.

A part of me, a knowing part,
a mockingly prophetic part,
has yet to abandon
the animal tribe of my youth.

Then I dream an underground crowd,
an enormous underworld crowd on the march.
Their bodies are thickets of shadow,
their legs an endless Bohemian wood.

So many flushed, exhausted middle-aged faces,
grim faces of miners, musicians, and executives,
sardined together there in close and hopeless darkness,
hard of breath and groaning, not even muttering
thin fibs of consolation to themselves.

Nearby, a throbbing edge is leaking to a constant flow
which might be surging hell's volcanic flood,
might be a river of decomposed sludge
or might not be an edge atall

but be the elliptical curve
where the protean crowd I don't own
with no beginning or end in my head

is always doubling doubling doubling doubling
doubling back
upon the treadmill of itself

in the mobius way
the whitecoats say
our universe does.

Irish History

for Paul Muldoon

Ah, Irish History
you remind me of Finbarr

whose pipe was like
Bogtown's once famously triple-shift factory

exhaling shape-shifting billows
of chemical smoke

floating over the neighbourhood
and in through the draftholes

to bedrooms of asthmatic children
sleeping three to a single

twenty-four hours a night.
Acceptably sick like the rest of us,

zig-zagging along the invincible
old roads, occasional new roads,

dodging boy racers
and delivery trucks.

Well, Finbarr, most of them anyway.
Planning to snuff somewhere cosy

and local with white puffy pillows, dry linen,
whispering sirens dressed up as nurses,

soft-chorusing rosary nuns
and docs that crack jokes

while pitting you into the blindness
in the middle of your forehead

where no-one can follow you,
out of your senses for good.

Then you went missing,
as in you ran out the door flootered,

screaming lighting abuse, and you never
came back to your fat daughter's lisp

and your conjoined triplet boys
(besides the nineteen who died),

your respectably chain-smoking wife,
your religious appearances

in the Pub on Sunday mornings
for rebel singsong and barrels of stout

with all the other veterans
of nothing much.

Two decades pass through the needle
of your vanishing.

Reports of you are unbelievably thin.
One punter claims he tagged you at Ascot

in 2006 in a scarf made of fox,
unpuffing an electronic cigarette,

hand in hand with your alternative,
extravagantly-hatted wife,

strolling along all at ease through the toffs;
also sporting your daughter,

the chef-de-partie and theatrical actress
and the son that's high up in the airforce.

But I know you are dying in dark visions and fits
in an abandoned industrial unit

on the outskirts of Manchester
with your rummaging Aberdeen girlfriend,

full of pills made in Hoxley and vintage vomit,
syphilis breeding with TB

inside you like those gigantic
pursuing Norvegicus

that swam in the wake
of your ferry, *Saint Patrick II*.

I'm one of those plague-driven rats
though you've seen

me on your travels as a mongrel
devouring a rabbit out by

the dump, an ox on the high-street,
a skybluish aura 'round an old medallion

sown into the pocket of the thirteenth-hand-coat
you got passed through the Sallies

by some long-dead slop-guzzler's
schizophrenic granny

whom the priest said – at the very small gathering
– had a special devotion to Mary.

I'm here to let you know that
your toothless Bogtown wife

might have set her hair on fire
in bed last night

but it didn't take as long as you might think.
Your daughter — who still misses you deeply —

is babbling away,
like an oracle of even less

having gone permanently
daft as well as half-blind

from plonk she goes stroking
one week from Aldi, Lidl the next,

besides being *Nana* to seventy-seven
(as well as ninety that died)

who've evolved from asthmatic
to an argot of spittle and cough.

You have one son left
because he hacked off the other two

with a saw
made of mother's lost teeth.

He had to — I know; sometimes
shard and excrement by chance or fate

or ecstasy will sprout
and shove the nethermost to light.

He seems to be recovering.
You won't be. Goodnight.

Notes for a Player

for Denis Boothman

i.

Towards the end you had hair made of moonlight.
Your sculptural face under moonlight.

October's incredible
new-minted radiance; Samhain's high moon
of the spirits. Too brilliant for winter.

White flare through the galloping mist.

Illumining Sugarloafs.

ii.

You knew everyday holy
and worshipped.

You knew communion as sharing abundance.

You knew music as a possible sanctity.

You knew time was confounded
by telling it slant.

You knew that worlds could return
in the stories

you plucked from your phases
and potted around.

iii.

As winter lacks
the Swallows' chirp
she lacks awake
in early dark
your free-given melody,
talk,
soothing her, lilting her up.
No lay from your shade now
but distant, anxious whispering
and she adrift
as leaf from oak
unrooted yet and
shelter lost,
security dissolved.
Shush now,
shush and halt
that bitter breath
like frost betongued
that she may sleep,
sleep down and deep
like a child on a quilt
in a summer of your warmth,
your blossoms softly calling.

You are the garden in her youth,
the Swallows in her longing.

iv.

Sunday in a nightgown at breakfast in Beech Grove/
Orsova LTD, where you are growing/grow
in your family/family business, phar-pharfing
– phar-phar-phar-phar – peeling a mandarin orange,

stirring your cuppa – ceramic ding ding –
humming along to McCormack or Callas,
tap-tapping shell – tap-tap again –
cracking open your ten AM free-range.

v.

We wish you eternal in Clifden in Summer,
Ashford in Autumn, Dublin in Winter, Venice in Spring.

vi.

In your after-dinner amphitheater
in Baile an Bhóthair,
under that suitably flickering
small chandelier
you grant our Venetian wish,
charming each adult/child squishing into
the bowl of your telling

to dismiss their belief
in an unhappy ending with
a reel from your old Dublin Am-Dram

or of your stretch in the Saudian desert
squatting on rugs in marquees in a moisture-less heat
sampling falafel, muttabaq, baklava,
swatting the flies with your wedding-ringed hand.

vii.

Backwards diving in the fashionable baths;
biking from Blackrock to horse-thronged Killarney
in the ration of your youth. Catholic glamour.

An Emergency beatnik in my mind,
observing tenderness, order and piety
all roads of your life

like Kerouac sober forever
on the way to Big Sur.

viii.

As if in pre-production, rehearsals,
as if only warming backstage of a five act
awaiting the usher's announcements;
as if only plotting with wrinkled OS
and biros the next epic hike.

ix.

I admire you brightly then, your glorious,
your tall last stand, Geronimo against oblivion.

x.

Minister of fleshandblood wordlaw,
transubstance of family tale.
Serenely bequeathing your memory's will.

Sharable story your pricelessly ultimate offspring.

xi.

Stories mobile, well-flexed and intent as those strong Kerry horses,
cantering along in the dapplement, untroubled in canopy dark,
steadily guiding their carriage, so weighty, so precious, of an almost
innocent love and endlessly fresh-sworn betrothment
around and around in the honeymoon waterfall park.

xii.

I knew that I was witness, for the first time in history, to the Standard of a Father who is dying.

xiii.

Climbed like a pilot your final ascent,
hauled on and drew deep through all that uphill heft
and atmospheric tapering of skyward days,
unembarrassed by the thirty-foot transparent tubing
taped to your rock-baldy, onetime thicketed upper lip,
splitting there into your nostrils and piping the dregs of your life,
a tentacle curling-uncurling obscenely behind you,
a deathspun silk, as you slouchingly, wheezingly, determinedly tread
forwards and backwards from kitchen/dining to a terminal
cabin-bed at the farther and farther corridor end,
attached under orders to a 3ft high air machine which 24/7
was dependably fanning and purring along to your rear
like your star-cruiser's idolising second mechanic or
a robot butler on your private submarine.

xiv.

Windows and mirrors must be hateful to the dying
who catch themselves paling away in the flashing at parties,
or see their own absence from next vacation's photographs
in the clinking of their hospice birthday glass
of Vino Rosso. Melancholy wisp-smile of those fitting on ghostliness.
Temptation to morphine pump yourself down into
the swallowhole of your own nothingness. Seeing right through
        yourself.
Your own transparence. Aquarium torso of finned heart,
        sawtoothed organs.

xv.

Yet you did not shrink from your blankening image
but flared into a magnified, mesmeric presence,
astounding all who gathered to your final stage,
com un plenilunio, violet and pink and enormous,
burning up space over Dalkey, Bull Harbour, Sandymount Strand,
astonishing lovers and traffic, the day before waning.

xvi.

Stage direction for the tragiparody called 'drawn-out-death':
If drizzle on our midnight scenery's unavoidable,
let it be rose-petal-showering
and let there be pulsing of moonbows as well.

xvii.

You have faults that you never become.
You become what is good in your gift.
Your grudges dissolve in a handshake;
your sorrows in joys you distribute like mints.

xviii.

In Padua some mornings you are whistling Puccini,
but in the long afternoons of oppressive humidity
death is an art-thief scaling your throat
intent on your tongue, intent on your singing.

xix.

Enter and stand operatic and floodlit on the last of your balconies,
arms stretched overhead, palms out, wiggling your rheumatic tips,
antennae of the opiate warmth, divining the evening's delight,
channeling what beams you receive to the milling piazza
beneath, winnowing…

…electing the grain of a grandchild who adores you
like ten thousand birthdays, like dicky-bowed Christmas
unwrapping always.

Gifting a lovebright identity.
Raising from the mass her individual face.

I bless this like a miracle.
I anoint it like the meaning of a saint.

xx.

Now she'll adore like us all in meandering dreams your
     true-mooring light,
moon-in-retreat reborn as a wandering star in the
     grand inner flight.

My Mother Speaks to Me of Suicide

My mother calls me up again to speak to me of suicide.
Another young man in the west has committed his suicide.
She tells me that I knew him in my teenage years
before I left home instead of killing myself
but I don't remember him at all.

Every single Irish week ten of us are doing it.
In my old town and dozens similar suicide's as regular
as weddings are. A plague, a scourge, an epidemic: I'm tired
of public platitudes like these. Not medicine nor scripture
can explain it; suicide at Irish rates is self-destruction
as mass movement, telling us the life we live,
all-of-us, here-and-now, has something
seriously wrong with it.

Here's a cliché with some life in it –
hope is what the spirit breathes.
Without it soul is drowning, tumbling
towards that bedrock of unfeelingness
we call the final resting place because
we cannot sink beyond it. Nor can we raise ourselves
from death, though each blind atom spinning free from
our decay will blend in turn with all there is
from starlight down to sucker-fish
in matter's everlasting carousel.

Alive and not unhappy now, and strolling through
my present neighbourhood towards Superquinn
for milk and bread, and chocolates or wine for my girlfriend,
I try to imagine my mother's distant face
as she speaks to me of suicide.

I image her framed in a darkness
like background in Dutch Renaissance portraits;
empty, yet dense; boundless, yet claustrophobic.

I see her haloed there by grotesque animations, miniature
pop-up-and-dissolve images of young men committing
their miniature suicides:

A young man hanging himself under a fag-butt moon
in a copse of old oaks in a town-centre park.

A young man hanging himself in his children's bedroom
so his children will find him that way
when they get home.

A young man OD-ing on his buddy's full phial of methadone
at Christmas in his mother's living-room.

A young man double-barrelly decapitating himself
in a cow shed;
the gun-roar submerged in the chaos of cows and machines.

A young man jumping into a fast-flowing river –
dead-cold-halt after zooming through
a three-day bender.

A young man jogging a dirt track leading up to a cliff,
then lepping off.

The hissing rocks, the witless fizzing of the sea.
The on-off beam of an automated lighthouse,
on, off, on, off, on…

A young man, sloshed, sliding sideways into a choppy reservoir
(two long-moored pleasure boats creaking there).

A young man choking himself on exhaust fumes
shortly after texting his final message
to the daughter he is not, with good reason,
allowed to go near.

A young man high-speeding his absurdly vroomed-up motorcar
into a midnight bend, staging it as an accident

so as to will the least mercy of a speakable grief
to those whom ceremony musters to attend.

From this bleak cinema inside my head, containing nothing
but herself, El Greco-style cartoons, and a landline telephone,
my mother, who has spent her whole life,
my mother, who has spent her whole eternity
surrounded, besieged by so many vainglorious, self-hating men
trying to get off the planet, calls up to speak to me of suicide,

with her Kerry accent cracking, her truth-parched accent cracking,
always verging though never quite breaking into a keen.

Yes, my mom calls me up every couple of weeks
to tell a fresh suicide I could easily be,
a fresh tomb I should statistically be buried in.

She calls and she calls and she tells and she tells,
as if she were the ledger of death self-inflicted
and I – her firstborn, the poet – a morbid accountant
who must reckon the substance, the meaning,
the worth of all this self-slaughter

but I can decipher no more
than this one thing so obvious and sure:
young men in Irish small towns and townlands,
suburbs and exurbs, flat-blocks and villages
are going to go right on killing themselves
until this life, this incredible life I adore
and which must not be wasted
be made worth living and living
and living again, for everyone.

Love commands the neighbourhood

for Karl Parkinson

Boy who bellows like the Friesians on a Monaghan hill,
boy who screeches like a martyr in the flame, love him.
Stunned woman in slippers and nightgown,
slouching a zig-zag to Superquinn,
scoring cider for herself, vodka for her bruiser, love her;

Indianinkman who on the night of his break out
smeared dog dirt on his neighbours' front doors,
hurled a brick through a little girl's window; him too.

Teenage thief who nicked your MacBook
in the park and in the cafe your keys
and will anyway die sometime tomorrow afternoon
in a glass or a powder.
Speeding mother
of four on her smartphone in the car
yet to crash into a toddler.
TY dealing molly and weed to the JCs
in the flytip on the banks of the Three Trouts streamborder
dividing private and council estates.

Drop-out student whacking the wall and the wardrobe
next door, trying to drown all his fatherly anger
in the well only he can be drowned in.
Croupy kids who will whoop through the walls
all the nights of the week.
All-hours alarms – electric hysterics
bansheeing silence, noisebombing calm;
Yakking mutts you want to throttle or drown.
Love all these.

Love them though they press you to white noise
and earplugs, though they edge you to codeine and dope.
They are helpless like you are, they are helpless like sorrow,
like anger, like love.

Chubby Thai always chuckling like
the chuckle-God's his brother
as he jogs after a football on the green.
Love the laughter and the boy, love the football
and the green, love the god and his brother.

Love the Ghost of the Pole who crashed into the wall.

Love the neighbour in a sari from Nairobi
who claims you spoke tongues in a warehouse
in Tallaght called The Victory Centre.
Love the door-to-door hawker who was born
in a hut in the drone-flattened Kush
and now parks his black beamer in front of
your western house, special-offering
bakemoulds and marbles and flyswats,
dispensing catalogues of flim-flam and gee-gaws
your daughter's absorbed in for hours.

Love all those with a love like a grieving,
for they too are leaving, they too are going their way.

Close by there's a man who stole through the barracks
after bombardment, collecting watches and teeth,
and a woman who walked out of a bomb. Love them.
Love fissures in footpaths that unspool overnight
like the nerve ends of an earthquake, or graph-lines
of impossible interest. Love the playground laid down
seven years from its promise, where youngsters
are pooling in twilight, nursing their secret new lives.
Love the road they call 'spine', and all the bright
yellow signs of advice that nobody follows.
Love the sexual nightscreams of cats, the boorish kaka-ing
of crows, lamp-posts they look down from
and assuredly outwait.

Love the first rough throat in the morning.
Love the last sad mutt in the night.

Photo: Catherine Boothman

DAVE LORDAN is the first writer to win Ireland's three national prizes for young poets. He is a former holder of the Ireland Chair of Poetry Bursary Award, the Kavanagh Award, and the Strong Award. He is a renowned performer of his own work, which the *Irish Times* called 'as brilliant on the page as it is in performance', and has read his work by invitation at festivals and venues across Europe and North America. His poems are regularly broadcast on Irish national radio and he is a contributing editor for Irish literary magazine, *The Stinging Fly*. He is a founding member and editor of experimental and cross-genre arts journal *Colony.ie*. He blogs on poetry and creativity at www.davelordanwriter.com. @vadenadrol